I0711871

Chapter 1: Understanding the Psychology of Motivation

Motivation is a complex psychological construct that drives behavior and influences the persistence of actions. To understand how to motivate people to go to fitness, it's essential to delve into the underlying psychological mechanisms. Theories such as Self-Determination Theory (SDT) and the Transtheoretical Model of Behavior Change provide valuable insights. SDT posits that motivation is fueled by three basic psychological needs: autonomy, competence, and relatedness. When these needs are met, individuals are more likely to engage in and maintain health-promoting behaviors such as exercise.

Autonomy refers to the feeling of being in control of one's actions, competence involves a sense of mastery and effectiveness, and relatedness is the need to connect with others. Fitness programs that emphasize these aspects can significantly enhance motivation. For example, offering a variety of workout options allows individuals to choose activities they enjoy, thereby increasing their sense of autonomy. Providing positive feedback and celebrating small achievements can boost feelings of competence, while creating a supportive community fosters relatedness.

Motivational interviewing is another powerful tool in understanding and enhancing fitness motivation. This client-centered counseling style helps individuals explore and resolve ambivalence toward exercise. By engaging in empathetic listening and reflective questioning, fitness professionals can help clients articulate their own reasons for change and strengthen their intrinsic motivation. This approach contrasts with traditional methods that rely on extrinsic motivators, such as rewards or punishments, which may not lead to sustained behavior change. Intrinsic motivation, which stems from personal satisfaction and enjoyment, is more likely to result in long-term commitment to fitness.

Another aspect to consider is the role of self-efficacy, or the belief in one's ability to succeed in specific situations. Self-efficacy influences how people think, feel, and act. High self-efficacy can enhance motivation by increasing confidence and resilience. Strategies to boost self-efficacy include setting achievable goals, celebrating small successes, and visualizing positive outcomes. For instance, a beginner might start with simple exercises and gradually increase the intensity and complexity as their confidence grows. Visualizing completing a workout successfully can also enhance self-efficacy and motivation.

Lastly, understanding the impact of habits and routines on motivation is crucial. Habits are behaviors that become automatic through repetition and can significantly influence motivation. Establishing a consistent fitness routine can help individuals overcome initial resistance and make exercise a regular part of their lives. Techniques such as habit stacking, where a new habit is linked to an existing one, can facilitate the development of healthy fitness habits. For example, someone might decide to go for a run immediately after their morning coffee, eventually making this sequence a natural part of their daily routine.

Chapter 2:
The Role of
Goal Setting

Setting specific, measurable, achievable, relevant, and time-bound (SMART) goals is a fundamental strategy for motivating individuals to engage in fitness. Goals provide direction, focus, and a sense of purpose. They help individuals track their progress and stay committed to their fitness journey. Effective goal setting involves breaking down long-term objectives into smaller, manageable tasks. For instance, instead of setting a vague goal like "get fit," a more effective approach would be to aim for "attend three gym sessions per week for the next month."

This specific goal is measurable, achievable, relevant, and time-bound. Additionally, it's important to set both outcome goals (e.g., losing 10 pounds) and process goals (e.g., working out for 30 minutes a day). Process goals focus on the behaviors necessary to achieve the desired outcome, making them more controllable and motivating. Regularly reviewing and adjusting goals based on progress and feedback ensures continuous motivation and prevents burnout.

Creating a visual representation of goals can further enhance motivation. Vision boards, fitness journals, and progress charts serve as constant reminders of what one is working towards. These tools help maintain focus and provide a sense of accomplishment as milestones are reached. For example, a vision board might include images of desired fitness outcomes, such as participating in a marathon or achieving a particular physique. Keeping a fitness journal where daily workouts, meals, and reflections are recorded can also provide valuable insights and track progress over time.

Incorporating rewards and incentives can also boost motivation. Celebrating small victories with non-food rewards, such as new workout gear or a relaxing massage, can reinforce positive behavior and keep individuals motivated. The key is to ensure that rewards are meaningful and aligned with fitness goals. For instance, rewarding oneself with a weekend hike for consistently hitting gym targets can further promote a healthy and active lifestyle.

Accountability partners and fitness coaches play a significant role in goal achievement. Sharing goals with a friend, family member, or coach can provide additional motivation and support. These individuals can offer encouragement, feedback, and a sense of accountability. Regular check-ins, whether in person or virtually, can help track progress and address any challenges that arise. For example, having a workout buddy can make exercise sessions more enjoyable and provide mutual motivation to stay committed.

Lastly, embracing flexibility in goal setting is crucial. Life is unpredictable, and rigid goals can sometimes lead to frustration and demotivation. It's important to recognize that setbacks and obstacles are part of the journey. Adjusting goals and plans when necessary, while maintaining a positive attitude, can help individuals stay on track. For instance, if a planned outdoor run is disrupted by bad weather, having an alternative indoor workout ready can ensure that fitness activities continue without interruption.

Chapter 3: Building a Supportive Community

A supportive community can significantly enhance motivation by providing social support, accountability, and a sense of belonging. Group fitness classes, online fitness communities, and workout buddies are effective ways to foster social connections. Being part of a fitness community creates a sense of shared purpose and commitment. For instance, joining a running club can provide encouragement, camaraderie, and a structured schedule that helps maintain motivation. Members of such communities can share their experiences, celebrate achievements, and provide support during challenging times.

Fitness communities can also offer a wealth of resources and knowledge. Experienced members and trainers can provide guidance on workout routines, nutrition, and injury prevention. Online forums and social media groups dedicated to fitness topics allow individuals to ask questions, share tips, and find inspiration. For example, a Facebook group for yoga enthusiasts might feature instructional videos, success stories, and motivational quotes that help members stay engaged and motivated.

Participating in group activities can add an element of fun and variety to fitness routines. Group classes such as Zumba, spinning, or boot camps offer structured workouts led by instructors who can motivate participants and ensure proper form. The social interaction and energy of a group setting can make exercise more enjoyable and less daunting. Additionally, friendly competition within a group can push individuals to challenge themselves and strive for their best performance.

Creating a sense of community within a fitness setting also involves fostering inclusivity and support. Ensuring that fitness environments are welcoming and non-judgmental is crucial. This includes offering classes and programs for different fitness levels and making accommodations for individuals with varying abilities. A supportive environment where everyone feels valued and respected can boost motivation and encourage long-term commitment. For instance, a gym that promotes a positive and inclusive culture will likely retain members who feel comfortable and supported in their fitness journey.

Technology plays a significant role in building and maintaining fitness communities. Fitness apps and wearable devices allow individuals to connect with others, share their progress, and participate in virtual challenges. Apps like Strava or MyFitnessPal enable users to log their workouts, track their progress, and engage with a broader fitness community. Virtual challenges, such as step competitions or online workout classes, provide additional motivation and a sense of connection, even when exercising alone.

Finally, organizing events and activities that promote community engagement can further enhance motivation. Charity runs, fitness retreats, and wellness workshops bring people together and provide opportunities to connect over shared interests. These events not only promote physical activity but also create lasting memories and friendships. For example, participating in a charity run for a cause one is passionate about can provide a powerful incentive to train and stay committed to fitness goals.

Chapter 4: Leveraging Technology for Motivation

Technology has revolutionized the fitness industry by providing innovative tools and resources to enhance motivation and engagement. Fitness apps, wearable devices, and online platforms offer personalized workout plans, real-time feedback, and social connectivity. Fitness apps like Fitbit, Nike Training Club, and Peloton provide a variety of workouts, from guided runs to yoga sessions, catering to different fitness levels and preferences. These apps often include features such as goal setting, progress tracking, and virtual challenges that help users stay motivated and accountable. For instance, a fitness app might offer a 30-day challenge that encourages users to complete daily workouts, providing a sense of achievement and progress.

Wearable devices such as smartwatches and fitness trackers monitor physical activity, heart rate, and sleep patterns, offering valuable insights into overall health and fitness. These devices provide real-time feedback, allowing users to adjust their workouts and ensure they are meeting their fitness goals. For example, a smartwatch might alert the user if their heart rate is too high during a workout, prompting them to slow down and avoid overexertion. Additionally, many wearables sync with fitness apps, providing a comprehensive view of one's fitness journey and progress.

Online fitness platforms and virtual training sessions have become increasingly popular, offering flexibility and convenience. Platforms like YouTube, Zoom, and various fitness websites provide access to a wide range of workout videos and live classes. Users can choose from a variety of exercise styles, from high-intensity interval training (HIIT) to Pilates, and participate in classes from the comfort of their homes. Virtual training sessions with personal trainers also provide personalized guidance and motivation, helping individuals stay on track and achieve their fitness goals.

Gamification is another effective strategy to enhance motivation through technology. Fitness games and apps that incorporate game-like elements, such as points, levels, and rewards, make exercise more engaging and enjoyable. Apps like Zombies, Run! turn workouts into interactive adventures, where users complete missions and earn rewards by running or walking. Gamification taps into the natural human desire for achievement and competition, providing a fun and motivating way to stay active.

Social media platforms and online communities offer additional motivation and support. Sharing fitness achievements, progress photos, and workout routines on platforms like Instagram, Facebook, and Twitter can provide a sense of accountability and encouragement. Engaging with fitness influencers, joining online fitness groups, and participating in virtual challenges create a sense of community and connection. For example, posting a workout video on Instagram and receiving positive feedback from followers can boost motivation and reinforce a commitment to fitness.

Moreover, virtual reality (VR) and augmented reality (AR) are emerging technologies that offer immersive and interactive fitness experiences. VR fitness games and simulations provide a fun and engaging way to exercise, allowing users to explore virtual worlds while working out. For instance, VR games like Beat Saber and Supernatural combine physical activity with immersive gameplay, making workouts enjoyable and motivating. AR apps can enhance outdoor activities by overlaying digital information, such as workout instructions or route guidance, onto the real world, providing an interactive and motivating experience.

Chapter 5: Overcoming Common Barriers to Fitness

Identifying and addressing common barriers to fitness is crucial for maintaining motivation and achieving long-term success. Common barriers include lack of time, physical limitations, financial constraints, and psychological obstacles. Understanding these barriers and implementing strategies to overcome them can help individuals stay committed to their fitness goals. For example, lack of time is a common barrier for many people. To overcome this, individuals can incorporate short, high-intensity workouts into their daily routines or break exercise into smaller, more manageable sessions throughout the day. Time management techniques, such as scheduling workouts in advance and treating them as non-negotiable appointments, can also help prioritize fitness.

Physical limitations, such as injuries or chronic conditions, can hinder fitness efforts. Adapting workouts to accommodate these limitations is essential. Consulting with healthcare professionals, such as physical therapists or fitness trainers, can provide guidance on safe and effective exercise modifications. For instance, individuals with joint issues might opt for low-impact activities like swimming or cycling instead of high-impact exercises like running. Using supportive equipment, such as braces or resistance bands, can also help prevent injury and enhance workout effectiveness.

Financial constraints can also be a barrier to fitness, particularly for those who cannot afford gym memberships or expensive equipment. However, many cost-effective or free fitness options are available. Bodyweight exercises, outdoor activities like running or hiking, and free online workout videos are all accessible ways to stay active without incurring significant costs. Community centers and local parks often offer free or low-cost fitness classes, providing opportunities for group exercise and social interaction. Additionally, investing in a few basic pieces of equipment, such as a yoga mat or resistance bands, can enable a wide range of home workouts.

Psychological obstacles, such as lack of confidence, fear of judgment, and low motivation, can also impede fitness efforts. Building self-confidence through gradual progress and celebrating small achievements can help overcome these barriers. For example, starting with beginner-friendly workouts and gradually increasing intensity can build confidence and a sense of accomplishment. Surrounding oneself with supportive and encouraging individuals, whether through workout buddies or online communities, can also alleviate fear of judgment and boost motivation. Developing a positive mindset and focusing on the benefits of exercise, such as improved mood and energy levels, can help maintain motivation.

Lastly, creating a supportive environment is essential for overcoming barriers to fitness. This includes organizing a dedicated workout space at home, setting up a schedule that accommodates regular exercise, and involving family and friends in fitness activities. A supportive environment reduces obstacles and makes it easier to maintain a consistent fitness routine. For instance, setting up a home gym with minimal equipment and ensuring it is easily accessible can eliminate the need for a gym membership and make regular workouts more convenient. Encouraging family members to join in fitness activities, such as family walks or group workouts, can also provide motivation and accountability.

Chapter 6: The Importance of Enjoyable Workouts

Enjoyable workouts are crucial for maintaining motivation and achieving long-term fitness goals. When exercise is enjoyable, it feels less like a chore and more like a rewarding and satisfying activity. Finding activities that align with personal interests and preferences can make fitness more appealing and sustainable. For instance, individuals who enjoy dancing might find Zumba classes or dance-based workout videos enjoyable and motivating. Similarly, those who love nature might prefer outdoor activities such as hiking, cycling, or running in scenic areas.

Variety is another key factor in keeping workouts enjoyable. Repeating the same routine can lead to boredom and decreased motivation. Incorporating a mix of different activities, such as strength training, cardio, yoga, and recreational sports, can keep workouts fresh and engaging. For example, alternating between gym sessions, outdoor runs, and yoga classes can provide a well-rounded fitness routine that prevents monotony. Experimenting with new fitness trends and activities, such as kickboxing, rock climbing, or aerial yoga, can also add excitement and keep motivation high.

Music is a powerful tool for enhancing workout enjoyment. Listening to upbeat and energizing music can boost mood, increase energy levels, and make exercise more enjoyable. Creating playlists with favorite songs or using music streaming services that offer workout-specific playlists can enhance the exercise experience. For instance, a high-energy playlist with fast-paced tracks can make a cardio session more enjoyable and help maintain a steady pace. Additionally, listening to podcasts or audiobooks during workouts can provide entertainment and mental stimulation, making the time pass more quickly.

Incorporating social elements into workouts can also enhance enjoyment. Exercising with friends, joining group fitness classes, or participating in fitness challenges with others can make workouts more fun and motivating. The social interaction and support from others create a positive and enjoyable workout environment. For example, participating in a weekly boot camp class with friends can provide a sense of camaraderie and make the workout more enjoyable. Social fitness apps that allow users to share their progress, participate in challenges, and support each other can also foster a sense of community and enhance workout enjoyment.

Rewarding oneself for completing workouts can further increase enjoyment and motivation. Small rewards, such as treating oneself to a favorite healthy snack, watching a favorite TV show, or enjoying a relaxing bath, can provide positive reinforcement for sticking to a fitness routine. The anticipation of a reward can make the workout experience more enjoyable and create a positive association with exercise. For instance, promising oneself a smoothie after a workout can serve as a motivating factor to complete the session.

Chapter 7: The Power of Habit Formation

Habits play a crucial role in maintaining a consistent fitness routine and achieving long-term fitness goals. Forming healthy habits involves creating automatic behaviors that become part of one's daily routine. The process of habit formation can be divided into three stages: cue, routine, and reward. Understanding and leveraging these stages can help individuals establish and maintain fitness habits. For instance, setting a specific cue, such as putting on workout clothes as soon as waking up, can trigger the routine of exercising. The reward can be the positive feelings and sense of accomplishment after completing the workout.

Consistency is key to habit formation. Repeating a behavior in the same context reinforces the habit loop and makes it more automatic over time. Establishing a consistent workout schedule, such as exercising at the same time each day, can help solidify the habit. For example, scheduling a workout session every morning before work can create a routine that becomes a natural part of the daily schedule. Using tools like calendars, reminders, and habit-tracking apps can also aid in maintaining consistency and tracking progress.

Starting with small, manageable habits can make the process of habit formation more achievable and less overwhelming. Gradually increasing the difficulty and intensity of workouts can build confidence and ensure sustainable progress. For instance, starting with a 10-minute daily walk and gradually increasing the duration and intensity can create a habit of regular physical activity. Celebrating small milestones and achievements along the way can provide motivation and reinforce the habit.

Creating a supportive environment is essential for successful habit formation. This includes organizing the physical environment to make healthy choices easier and more convenient. For example, setting up a designated workout space at home, keeping workout clothes and equipment easily accessible, and minimizing distractions can facilitate the habit of regular exercise. Surrounding oneself with supportive and encouraging individuals can also provide motivation and accountability. Sharing fitness goals and progress with friends, family, or a workout buddy can create a sense of commitment and support.

Identifying and addressing potential obstacles and barriers is crucial for maintaining fitness habits. Planning for setbacks and having strategies in place to overcome them can ensure long-term success. For example, having alternative workout options for days when the planned activity is not possible, such as indoor workouts for rainy days, can prevent disruptions to the fitness routine. Developing a flexible mindset and recognizing that occasional setbacks are part of the process can help maintain motivation and commitment.

Chapter 8: Personalizing Fitness Plans

Personalizing fitness plans is essential for ensuring that exercise routines are effective, enjoyable, and sustainable. Individual preferences, goals, fitness levels, and physical conditions vary, so a one-size-fits-all approach is unlikely to be successful. Tailoring fitness plans to meet individual needs and preferences can enhance motivation and adherence. For example, someone who enjoys social interaction might prefer group fitness classes or team sports, while someone who values solitude might prefer running or home workouts.

Personalized fitness plans should take into account individual goals and objectives. Whether the goal is weight loss, muscle gain, improved endurance, or overall health, the fitness plan should be designed to achieve these specific outcomes. Setting realistic and achievable goals based on individual capabilities and progress is essential. For instance, a beginner might set an initial goal of completing a 5K run, while a more experienced athlete might aim for a marathon.

Assessing current fitness levels and physical conditions is crucial for creating personalized fitness plans. Fitness assessments, such as measuring body composition, cardiovascular endurance, strength, and flexibility, provide valuable information for designing effective workouts. Consulting with fitness professionals, such as personal trainers or physiotherapists, can provide expert guidance and ensure that the fitness plan is safe and effective. For example, a fitness assessment might reveal that someone has weak core muscles, prompting the inclusion of specific core strengthening exercises in the workout routine.

Incorporating a variety of exercises and activities can enhance the effectiveness and enjoyment of personalized fitness plans. Balancing different types of exercise, such as cardio, strength training, flexibility, and balance exercises, ensures a well-rounded fitness routine. For instance, a weekly fitness plan might include running for cardiovascular health, weightlifting for strength, yoga for flexibility, and balance exercises to prevent injury. Varying the types of exercises and incorporating new activities can also prevent boredom and keep motivation high.

Adjusting fitness plans based on progress and feedback is essential for continuous improvement and motivation. Regularly reviewing and modifying the plan based on individual progress, preferences, and changing goals ensures that the fitness routine remains effective and enjoyable. For example, if someone finds that their current workout routine is no longer challenging or enjoyable, incorporating new exercises or increasing the intensity can reignite motivation and ensure continued progress.

Chapter 9:
The Impact of Nutrition on Fitness Motivation

Nutrition plays a vital role in fitness motivation and overall success. A balanced and nutritious diet provides the energy and nutrients necessary for optimal performance and recovery. Proper nutrition can enhance workout effectiveness, prevent fatigue, and support muscle growth and repair. Understanding the connection between nutrition and fitness can help individuals make informed dietary choices that support their fitness goals. For instance, consuming a balanced meal with adequate protein, carbohydrates, and healthy fats before a workout can provide the energy needed for optimal performance. Post-workout nutrition, such as a protein-rich snack, supports muscle recovery and growth.

Hydration is another crucial aspect of nutrition that impacts fitness motivation and performance. Staying adequately hydrated before, during, and after workouts is essential for maintaining energy levels, preventing dehydration, and supporting overall health. Drinking water throughout the day and incorporating hydrating foods, such as fruits and vegetables, into the diet can ensure proper hydration. For example, drinking water before a workout and sipping water during exercise can prevent dehydration and maintain performance.

Meal timing and frequency also play a role in fitness motivation and performance. Eating smaller, balanced meals and snacks throughout the day can help maintain steady energy levels and prevent hunger-induced fatigue. Planning meals and snacks around workout times can enhance energy availability and support optimal performance. For instance, eating a small snack, such as a banana or a handful of nuts, before a workout can provide a quick energy boost, while a balanced meal after exercise can support recovery and replenish energy stores.

Incorporating a variety of nutrient-dense foods into the diet can enhance overall health and fitness. Nutrient-dense foods, such as fruits, vegetables, whole grains, lean proteins, and healthy fats, provide essential vitamins, minerals, and antioxidants that support overall health and fitness. For example, incorporating a variety of colorful fruits and vegetables into meals can provide a wide range of nutrients that support immune function, energy production, and overall well-being.

Addressing specific dietary needs and preferences is essential for personalized nutrition and fitness plans. Individuals with specific dietary preferences, such as vegetarian, vegan, or gluten-free diets, should ensure they are meeting their nutritional needs while supporting their fitness goals. Consulting with a registered dietitian or nutritionist can provide expert guidance and personalized recommendations. For example, a vegan athlete might focus on plant-based protein sources, such as legumes, tofu, and quinoa, to support muscle growth and recovery.

Chapter 10: The Influence of Sleep and Recovery

Sleep and recovery are critical components of fitness motivation and overall success. Adequate sleep and proper recovery support physical and mental well-being, enhance workout performance, and prevent injury. Understanding the importance of sleep and recovery and implementing effective strategies can enhance fitness motivation and outcomes. For instance, getting 7-9 hours of quality sleep each night supports optimal physical and cognitive function, allowing for better performance during workouts. Establishing a consistent sleep routine, such as going to bed and waking up at the same time each day, can improve sleep quality and support overall health.

Recovery practices, such as stretching, foam rolling, and rest days, are essential for preventing injury and supporting muscle repair and growth. Incorporating regular recovery practices into a fitness routine can enhance performance and prevent burnout. For example, incorporating a stretching routine after workouts can improve flexibility, reduce muscle soreness, and prevent injury. Foam rolling can help release muscle tension and improve blood flow, supporting muscle recovery and reducing the risk of injury.

Active recovery, such as low-intensity activities and light exercise, can also support recovery and enhance overall fitness. Activities like walking, swimming, or gentle yoga can promote blood flow and aid in muscle recovery without placing excessive strain on the body. For instance, taking a leisurely walk or practicing gentle yoga on rest days can support recovery and maintain physical activity levels.

Listening to the body and recognizing the signs of overtraining is crucial for preventing injury and maintaining motivation. Overtraining can lead to physical and mental fatigue, decreased performance, and increased risk of injury. Paying attention to signs such as persistent muscle soreness, fatigue, and decreased motivation can help identify when rest and recovery are needed. Adjusting workout intensity, incorporating rest days, and prioritizing recovery can prevent overtraining and support long-term fitness success.

Implementing relaxation and stress management techniques can also enhance sleep quality and recovery. Practices such as meditation, deep breathing, and mindfulness can reduce stress and promote relaxation, supporting better sleep and overall well-being. For example, incorporating a short meditation or deep breathing exercise before bed can improve sleep quality and support overall health.

Chapter 11: The Role of Positive Reinforcement

Positive reinforcement is a powerful tool for enhancing fitness motivation and achieving long-term success. Reinforcing positive behaviors with rewards and encouragement can create a positive association with exercise and reinforce commitment to fitness goals. Understanding the principles of positive reinforcement and implementing effective strategies can boost motivation and support consistent fitness efforts. For instance, rewarding oneself with a favorite healthy treat, new workout gear, or a relaxing activity after reaching a fitness milestone can provide motivation and a sense of accomplishment.

Using positive self-talk and affirmations can also enhance motivation and reinforce positive behaviors. Encouraging oneself with positive statements, such as "I am strong and capable" or "I can achieve my fitness goals," can boost confidence and motivation. For example, repeating positive affirmations before a workout can enhance mental focus and motivation, making the exercise experience more enjoyable and effective.

Celebrating small victories and progress is essential for maintaining motivation and reinforcing positive behaviors. Recognizing and celebrating achievements, such as completing a challenging workout or reaching a fitness milestone, can provide a sense of accomplishment and motivate continued effort. For example, tracking progress with a fitness journal and celebrating each milestone, such as increasing workout intensity or achieving a weight loss goal, can provide motivation and reinforce positive behaviors.

Providing positive feedback and encouragement to oneself and others can also boost motivation and support fitness efforts. Offering praise and recognition for effort and progress can create a positive and motivating environment. For instance, complimenting a workout buddy on their progress and effort can provide encouragement and reinforce commitment to fitness goals. Similarly, recognizing and appreciating one's own efforts and achievements can boost self-confidence and motivation.

Creating a positive and supportive environment is crucial for reinforcing positive behaviors and maintaining motivation. Surrounding oneself with encouraging and supportive individuals, such as workout buddies, fitness coaches, and supportive friends and family, can provide motivation and accountability. For example, joining a supportive fitness community or group can create a positive environment that reinforces commitment to fitness goals.

Chapter 12: The Benefits of Mindfulness and Mental Focus

Mindfulness and mental focus play a significant role in enhancing fitness motivation and achieving long-term success. Practicing mindfulness involves being fully present and engaged in the current moment, which can enhance the exercise experience and improve performance. Understanding the benefits of mindfulness and mental focus and incorporating mindfulness practices into fitness routines can boost motivation and support overall well-being. For example, practicing mindfulness during workouts, such as paying attention to breathing, body sensations, and movements, can enhance focus and performance.

Mindfulness practices, such as meditation and deep breathing, can reduce stress and improve mental clarity, supporting better decision-making and motivation. Incorporating mindfulness practices into daily routines can enhance overall well-being and support fitness efforts. For instance, practicing a short meditation or deep breathing exercise before a workout can improve mental focus and motivation, making the exercise experience more enjoyable and effective.

Setting intentions and practicing visualization can also enhance mental focus and motivation. Setting a clear intention for each workout, such as focusing on a specific goal or aspect of performance, can improve focus and motivation. Visualization techniques, such as imagining oneself completing a workout successfully or achieving a fitness goal, can boost confidence and motivation. For example, visualizing completing a challenging workout or achieving a personal best can enhance mental focus and motivation during the exercise.

Incorporating mindfulness into fitness routines can also enhance the mind-body connection and improve overall performance. Paying attention to body sensations, movements, and alignment can improve form and prevent injury. For instance, practicing mindfulness during yoga or strength training can enhance body awareness and ensure proper form and technique. This improved mind-body connection can lead to better performance and reduced risk of injury.

Mindfulness practices can also enhance recovery and overall well-being. Practicing mindfulness techniques, such as meditation, deep breathing, and body scanning, can promote relaxation and reduce stress, supporting better recovery and overall health. For example, incorporating a short mindfulness practice after a workout can promote relaxation and aid in muscle recovery.

Chapter 13: The Impact of Environmental Factors

Environmental factors play a significant role in fitness motivation and overall success. The physical and social environment can influence exercise behaviors and motivation. Understanding the impact of environmental factors and creating a supportive and motivating environment can enhance fitness efforts. For example, creating a designated workout space at home, ensuring it is well-equipped and free of distractions, can make exercise more convenient and enjoyable. Organizing workout equipment, setting up motivational posters, and ensuring adequate lighting can create a positive and motivating workout environment.

Outdoor environments can also influence fitness motivation and enjoyment. Exercising in natural settings, such as parks, trails, or beaches, can enhance the exercise experience and provide additional health benefits. For instance, running or cycling in a scenic park can boost mood and motivation, making the workout more enjoyable. The fresh air, natural scenery, and exposure to sunlight can enhance overall well-being and support fitness efforts.

The social environment, including the presence of supportive and encouraging individuals, can also impact fitness motivation. Surrounding oneself with positive and supportive individuals, such as workout buddies, fitness coaches, and supportive friends and family, can provide motivation and accountability. For example, joining a fitness group or class can create a sense of community and support, making exercise more enjoyable and motivating.

Creating a positive and supportive work environment can also enhance fitness efforts. Encouraging workplace wellness programs, providing opportunities for physical activity, and promoting a healthy work-life balance can support overall well-being and fitness motivation. For example, offering on-site fitness classes, organizing walking meetings, and providing incentives for physical activity can create a supportive work environment that encourages regular exercise.

Addressing and minimizing environmental barriers to fitness is essential for maintaining motivation and achieving long-term success. Identifying and addressing barriers, such as lack of access to fitness facilities, unsafe neighborhoods, or extreme weather conditions, can help create a more supportive environment. For instance, finding alternative workout options, such as home workouts or indoor fitness classes, can overcome barriers related to weather or safety. Creating a safe and supportive neighborhood environment, such as improving lighting and promoting community fitness events, can also enhance fitness motivation and participation.

Chapter 14: The Role of Goal Setting and Planning

Goal setting and planning are critical components of fitness motivation and success. Setting clear, specific, and achievable goals provides direction and purpose, enhancing motivation and commitment. Understanding the principles of effective goal setting and implementing goal-setting strategies can boost motivation and support long-term success. For example, setting SMART goals (Specific, Measurable, Achievable, Relevant, and Time-bound) can provide a clear and structured approach to achieving fitness objectives. For instance, setting a goal to "run a 5K in 30 minutes within three months" is a specific and measurable goal that provides a clear target and timeline.

Breaking down larger goals into smaller, manageable steps can make the process of achieving fitness goals more achievable and less overwhelming. Setting short-term goals that lead to the achievement of long-term objectives can provide a sense of progress and motivation. For example, breaking down the goal of running a marathon into smaller goals, such as increasing weekly mileage or improving running pace, can provide a structured and motivating approach.

Creating a detailed fitness plan that outlines specific actions, timelines, and milestones can enhance motivation and accountability. A well-structured plan provides a clear roadmap for achieving fitness goals and ensures that progress is tracked and monitored. For example, creating a weekly workout schedule that includes specific exercises, durations, and intensity levels can provide structure and direction. Regularly reviewing and adjusting the fitness plan based on progress and feedback ensures that the plan remains effective and motivating.

Tracking progress and celebrating achievements are essential for maintaining motivation and reinforcing positive behaviors. Using tools such as fitness journals, apps, or wearable devices to track workouts, progress, and milestones can provide valuable feedback and motivation. For example, using a fitness app to log workouts and monitor progress can provide a visual representation of achievements and motivate continued effort. Celebrating milestones and achievements, such as completing a fitness challenge or reaching a personal best, can provide a sense of accomplishment and reinforce commitment to fitness goals.

Incorporating accountability measures, such as sharing goals and progress with a workout buddy, coach, or online community, can enhance motivation and support. Sharing goals and progress creates a sense of commitment and accountability, making it more likely to stay on track. For example, joining an online fitness community and participating in challenges and discussions can provide support, motivation, and accountability.

Chapter 15: The Long-Term Benefits of Fitness Motivation

Maintaining fitness motivation and achieving long-term success offers numerous physical, mental, and emotional benefits. Regular physical activity improves overall health, reduces the risk of chronic diseases, enhances mental well-being, and boosts energy levels. Understanding the long-term benefits of fitness motivation can provide additional motivation and reinforce commitment to a fitness routine. For example, regular exercise can reduce the risk of heart disease, diabetes, and certain cancers, supporting overall health and longevity.

Fitness motivation also enhances mental health and well-being. Regular physical activity reduces stress, anxiety, and depression, improves mood, and boosts cognitive function. For instance, engaging in regular aerobic exercise, such as running or cycling, can release endorphins and improve mood, providing mental health benefits. The sense of accomplishment and confidence gained from achieving fitness goals can also enhance self-esteem and overall well-being.

Long-term fitness motivation supports healthy habits and behaviors beyond physical activity. Individuals committed to fitness are more likely to adopt healthy dietary habits, prioritize sleep and recovery, and engage in other wellness practices. For example, someone motivated to maintain a regular fitness routine might also prioritize a balanced diet, adequate sleep, and stress management techniques, supporting overall health and well-being.

Fitness motivation fosters a positive and proactive approach to health and well-being. Individuals motivated to stay active and healthy are more likely to take preventive measures, seek regular health check-ups, and engage in health-promoting behaviors. For instance, someone committed to fitness might also prioritize regular medical check-ups, vaccinations, and other preventive health measures, supporting overall health and longevity.

Maintaining fitness motivation and achieving long-term success can also inspire and motivate others. Individuals who demonstrate commitment and dedication to fitness can serve as role models and encourage others to adopt healthy habits. For example, a parent who maintains a regular fitness routine can inspire their children to be active and prioritize their health. Similarly, sharing fitness achievements and progress on social media or within a community can motivate others to pursue their fitness goals.

In conclusion, understanding and leveraging the principles of fitness motivation can enhance the exercise experience, support long-term success, and improve overall health and well-being. By addressing common barriers, personalizing fitness plans, incorporating positive reinforcement, and recognizing the benefits of mindfulness, nutrition, and recovery, individuals can maintain motivation and achieve their fitness goals. Creating a supportive environment, setting clear goals, and celebrating achievements further reinforce commitment and enhance the overall fitness journey.